The author is grateful to the many people who helped him in the preparation of this book, providing background information and photographs. These include Albert M. Monaco, Jr., U.S. Volleyball Association; John Roberts, National Federation of State High School Associations; Jane Habiger, Association of Intercollegiate Athletics for Women; Nick Curran, International Volleyball Association; Becky Kummerfeld, University of Southern California; Herb Field, Herb Field Art Studios; Gary Wagner, Wagner International Photos; Gina Maher, and Bill Sullivan.

Special thanks are offered Pat Hicks, coach of the girls' volleyball team at Hastings High School, Hastings-on-Hudson, New York, and these members of the team who posed for photographs: Hanni Dorn, Monica Guttmann, Sarah Callahan, Julie Pennington, Kerry Schmidt, Bronwyn Eaton, Catherine Cugliari, Merry Young, Suzy Hopkins, Rosemary Kuhn, Sharon Bloom, Carol Tino, Gail Gustafson, Kathy Finnegan, and also Michael Drumm.

JAPAN
JAPAN
4
JAPAN
1
11
12

BETTER VOLLEYBALL *for Girls*

George Sullivan

DODD, MEAD & COMPANY · NEW YORK

Frontispiece: U.S. Women's National Volleyball Team is one of the world's best. Here team members form wall of blockers to prevent championship Japanese women's team from scoring.

Copyright © 1979 by George Sullivan
All rights reserved
No part of this book may be reproduced in any form
without permission in writing from the publisher
Printed in the United States of America

1 2 3 4 5 6 7 8 9 10

Library of Congress Cataloging in Publication Data

Sullivan, George, 1927–
    Better volleyball for girls.

    SUMMARY: An introduction to women's volleyball,
including discussions of its growth in popularity,
how it is played, the style of play today, and the
difference in women's and men's volleyball.
    1. Volleyball for women—History—Juvenile literature.
2. Volleyball—Juvenile literature. [1. Volleyball]
I. Title.
GV1015.4.W66S9   796.32'5   79-12640
ISBN 0-396-07697-1

CONTENTS

THE "NEW" VOLLEYBALL

During a game in the women's international volleyball championships not long ago, Debbie Green, then in her mid-teens, dove headfirst to make a save, dug the ball up into the air with her forearms, landed on her hands and chest, then went sliding along the floor on her belly.

"Wow!" said a sportscaster covering the game. "That girl has taken quite a fall. Let's hope she can stay in the game."

The sportscaster didn't realize that Debbie's "fall" was an accepted piece of strategy. Before the game was over, every player on the American team went plunging to the floor in much the same manner several times.

Volleyball used to be regarded as a "pitty-pat" sport, with opposing teams gently lobbing the ball back and forth over the net. In terms of action and excitement, the game compared with tossing a beanbag or darts.

Not any more. The game today features diving saves—like those performed by Debbie Green and her teammates—and rolling digs. In the last named, a player rolls over on one shoulder after retrieving the ball, and rebounds to her feet in time for the next play.

The spike is probably the chief hallmark of modern volleyball, or what's often referred to as *power* volleyball. A player leaps high to slam the ball down

As teenager, Debbie Green starred for U.S. Women's National Team.

No longer is volleyball a pitty-pat sport.

hard into the opposition court. Sometimes it's hit so hard, the ball seems as if it is going to nail the closest defensive player to the floor.

But defending players have learned to cope with even the most devastating spikings, rising up to block the ball just as it comes across the net. Should a spiked ball pierce the forward defensive line, a back-court player will handle it with a deft forearm pass, called a bump.

No one knows for sure how many people participate in volleyball in the United States. The Athletic Institute says that 60 million Americans play the game at one time or another during the year. That figure is probably as good as any other. One thing

Grace and timing are still important.

is certain: Volleyball is more popular today than ever before in its history.

The exciting fun the game offers is the chief reason. But there are several others. Anyone can play volleyball. One's size isn't important; girls who are not much more than 5-feet tall can leap up and spike the ball, or block it when someone else does.

If you prefer not to spike, you can be a setter, setting up the ball so it can be spiked by a team-mate. Setting takes a deft touch.

Volleyball can be played just about anywhere, indoors or out. All you need is a ball, a net, and something which to tie it to.

Another plus is that girls and boys can play to-gether on the same team, a claim few other sports can make.

"Volleyball—power volleyball—is a great sport," says one coach. "It belongs right up there with track and field and soccer, baseball, and football—any sport you care to name."

In 1895, William G. Morgan became director of the YMCA (Young Men's Christian Association) in Holyoke, Massachusetts. He had not been in his new job very long when he saw the need for some new form of recreation for his physical education classes, which were growing in size and enthusiasm.

Morgan rejected basketball (which had been "in-vented" in nearby Springfield only four years before) because it was too rough.

"Birthplace of Volleyball" proclaims sign as you enter Holyoke, Massachusetts.

Then tennis occurred to him. But since tennis required rackets, nets, and balls, yet could be played by only a limited number of people, he decided against that sport.

He liked the idea of using a net and hitting a ball

back and forth across it. You really didn't have to use a racket, Morgan reasoned; players could simply hit the ball with their hands or fists.

Getting a ball of the right size and weight was a problem. When a basketball was tried, it was found to be too heavy.

Morgan next experimented with the inflated inner lining of a basketball, called a bladder. But that proved too light.

"Finally, we decided that a ball made along the lines of the present volleyball was what was needed," Morgan wrote in later years. He asked A. G. Spalding, a sporting goods manufacturer in neighboring Chicopee, to make a ball according to his specifications. "It gave satisfaction," Morgan said.

Morgan's first set of rules established the game's essential ingredients: It was to be played in a rectangular court between two opposing teams that attempted to hit the ball back and forth across a high net until it touched the floor or was knocked out of bounds.

Games, however, were played in innings. An inning consisted of three serves by each team.

The top of the net was a mere 6 feet, 6 inches from the floor, because Morgan wanted it "just above the average man's head." The number of hits per side was not limited.

Morgan thought his new game resembled badminton, so he called it "mintonette." But that name lasted only a year or so. During an exhibition game at Springfield College, a Springfield professor suggested it be called "volley ball" (it was two words then, not one).

Morgan had no desire to profit from the game. He was only interested in sharing it with as many people as possible. In 1896, he staged an exhibition game for the annual convention of the YMCA physical directors. Afterward, when the physical directors went to him and asked for more information and a set of rules, Morgan was happy to oblige.

The following year, 1897, the first official rules were published in the "Handbook of the Athletic League of the YMCAs of North America."

Because most of the public gymnasiums in the country were operated by the YMCA at the time, it was that organization that spearheaded the game's growth and development. Not only did YMCA physical education directors introduce volleyball in most sections of the United States, but in many foreign countries as well.

In 1913, the Reverend F. H. Brown, an American missionary, began teaching volleyball in Japan, organizing teams at the Tokyo YMCA. The game became popular in Japan at office and factory lunch breaks. Spinning companies, where workers were mostly women, organized teams by the hundreds. Japanese teenagers began playing volleyball in physical education classes and at school recess periods. In time, volleyball would become one of Japan's most important sports.

Outdoor volleyball at Smith College in 1918.

Back in the United States, the rules for volleyball kept changing, almost on a year-by-year basis. In 1916, the concept of innings was abolished in favor of a game of 15 points. Players were not permitted to play the ball a second time.

That same year, the *Volleyball Official Guide* estimated that 200,000 Americans were playing the game. During World War I, the sport proved a popular recreation activity for American forces in Europe.

The game's rules continued to be revised. The rule that the ball can be hit only three times on each side of the net was introduced in 1920. Two years later, the first national volleyball championships were held. A Brooklyn, New York, YMCA was the scene, with 23 teams competing. A Pittsburgh "Y" emerged the winner.

Despite this activity, volleyball did not begin to develop as a sport for girls and women until fairly recent times. After all, the game was thought up by a YMCA physical director, and the sport was advanced by the YMCA through the first decades of the 1900s. And YMCA stands for Young *Men's* Christian Association. Women weren't even allowed to use YMCA gymnasiums or other facilities in the organization's early years.

The first rules for women's volleyball weren't published until 1924, although some women's schools and colleges played the sport before that time. The 1924 rules called for a lower net than was being used in the men's version of the game at the time, and, instead of playing for 15 points, the game for women was divided into halves, each 20 minutes in length. It was felt that women were too delicate to take part in the frantic play that could occur when a game was tied at 14-14 and teams were battling to score the winning point.

Women weren't expected to excel in sports in those days. When, in 1928, an instruction book, *Volleyball for Women*, was published, the book's introduction advised readers, "The average college girl will never become an expert in the game . . . ."

The sport was recommended to girls because it was thought to be an aid to good posture, a corrective exercise for what was called "student stoop." The most popular instruction book of the day was titled *Volley Ball, a Man's Game*.

Of course, all of this was to change. But it took time.

The United States Volleyball Association was founded in 1928, and it has served as the sport's

Volleyball uniforms of the 1950s often featured short skirts like these.

Volleyball is a major sport in Japan. Here high school girls play during recess.

governing body since that time. The USVBA conducts the annual national championships, publishes the game's official rule book, and certifies volleyball officials. Beginning in 1949, the USVBA began holding an annual championship tournament for women.

Although volleyball continued to grow in popularity in the United States, it never gained widespread popularity as a competitive sport. Volleyball was a game you played at picnics or in the backyard at family gatherings. "It was right up there with Frisbee and the three-legged race," one observer noted.

This wasn't true in other countries, however. In Poland, Cuba, Russia, and Japan, men's and women's teams played a tough, demanding version of the game.

Because of its international popularity, volleyball was chosen as an Olympic sport in 1964. The Games were held in Japan that year, so Japanese athletes were more determined than ever to perform well.

Japanese women unveiled a type of volleyball that caused spectators and opponents to gape in amazement. They emphasized fundamentals, with every player able to execute every type of pass and spike with machinelike precision.

But more than that, the Japanese women stressed agility. They were quick and fast. They dove for the ball and rolled on the floor.

"Kamikaze volleyball," is what one observer called it. (During World War II, a Japanese pilot trained to make a suicide crash was called a kamikaze.)

Japanese women won the Olympic gold medal that year (and they won it again in 1976). Thanks to television and their tours of foreign countries, the Japanese women's team and their electrifying style became known throughout the world.

American women, like those in other countries, were enormously influenced by the playing style of the Japanese.

That wasn't all that was happening. During the late 1960s and early 1970s, American women began to take a much more active role in all sports. This new attitude was supported by Congressional lawmakers who, in 1972, passed legislation that stated: No person in the United States shall, on the basis of sex, be excluded from participation in, be denied the benefits of, or be subjected to discrimination under any education program or activity re-

ceiving Federal financial assistance . . ."

This law meant that school and college athletic programs had to offer equal opportunities for boys and girls. For women's sports, a period of mushrooming growth followed. Volleyball was one of the sports to benefit the most.

During the 1968-69 school year, 3,312 high schools offered intrescholastic volleyball competition. By the year 1978, the number had increased to 11,690 schools. The number of players surged from 59,132 to 326,091 during the same period. That's an increase of more than 500 percent. In addition, there are hundreds of thousands of high

Japanese women are all smiles after defeating American team during 1978 exhibition tour.

More than 700 colleges offer intercollegiate volleyball for women. These blockers represent the powerful University of Southern California team.

school girls who play volleyball as a club, class, or intramural activity.

There are well over 700 colleges that offer varsity volleyball programs for girls, according to the Association for Intercollegiate Athletics for Women. In this respect, volleyball is second only to basketball, outranking tennis, swimming and diving, and track and field.

Professional volleyball became a reality in 1975 with the founding of the International Volleyball Association. Its teams are based largely in cities of the Southwest and Pacific Coast. What's noteworthy about the IVA is that its teams are co-ed, that is, made up of both men and women players. You may not be able to see a woman playing linebacker for

Sue Caldwell is a pro headliner for Los Angeles franchise of the International Volleyball Association.

the Dallas Cowboys or first base for the New York Yankees, but you can cheer for a woman spiking the ball for such volleyball teams as the Orange County Stars or the Phoenix Heat.

In southern California, beach volleyball is enormously popular. Don't think that just because it's a game played by barefooted people wearing swim suits that beach volleyball is unorganized or even informal. The California Beach Volleyball Association, organized in 1976, conducts volleyball tournaments every weekend from May to September, beginning in Santa Cruz and moving south to include Sorrento, Santa Monica, Hermosa, and Corona del Mar. A tournament at Will Rogers State Park beach drew 7,000 fans not long ago.

"It's almost a religion" is how one veteran player describes beach volleyball. "The feeling you get after being on the beach all day is phenomenal. There's the hot sun, great exercise, and an ocean to dive into. There's no better feeling."

Volleyball is also a popular beach game in Hawaii, Florida, Virginia, and at Davis Park on Fire Island in New York.

But to most New Yorkers, volleyball is a park game. In the Sheep Meadow in Central Park, nets go up around noon on Saturdays and Sundays and come down at dusk. ("If you leave a net up overnight," says one park player, "it's gone in the morning.") At the height of the outdoor season, there are four or five games going on at once.

Teams are co-ed, although women aren't encouraged to play on the center court, where the most ferocious games take place. The men say they're worried about injuring the women with a spike.

No matter where it is played—in a park, on the beach, or in a gym—and no matter who happens to be playing, from young high schoolers to professional veterans, strategy is much the same, teams using their three hits in this manner:

The first hit is a pass to the setter.

The second hit is the set, which "sets up" the spiker.

The third hit is the spike.

"Volleyball is speed, fitness, discipline, and, most of all, it's timing," says Arie Selinger, coach of the U.S. Women's National Volleyball Team.

"There's no time to waste, as in other sports. It's now or never. The ball comes to you and you'd better know what to do. There are five other people depending on you. And you have to depend on yourself for everything."

William Morgan, the man who thought up volleyball, died in 1942. His idea had been that volleyball should be a game of exercise and fun. He never thought of it as a competitive sport.

Volleyball is still a game of exercise and fun, of course. But excitement and thrills have been added. What's happened surely would have astonished Mr. Morgan.

CLOTHING AND EQUIPMENT

Just as the game of volleyball itself has changed in recent years, so has the clothing and equipment for the sport.

The biggest changes have involved footwear, that is, sneakers. There are dozens of styles to choose from, whereas there used to be only a few.

In the case of sneakers for volleyball, the built-up portion of the sneaker that supports the ankle—called the collar—is important. The collar should be padded with smooth leather and be high enough to protect the ankle and the Achilles' tendon.

There should be plenty of cushioning within the sole. Arch support is important, too.

Sneakers are available in many different materials. Those made of polyester and nylon will last the longest. Leather and suede sneakers are both comfortable and durable, but they're the most expensive. Nylon and nylon mesh wear well and are light in weight. Nonporous vinyl sneakers tend to make your feet sweat.

Some of the leading sports shoe manufacturers —Adidas, Puma, and Tiger among them—offer special volleyball sneakers. These can be quite expensive, however, ranging up to $40. Most basketball sneakers, or those meant for almost any indoor court game, are fine for volleyball.

Whatever type you buy, just be sure they're light, durable, and comfortable. Ridged or rippled gumrubber soles will enable you to make the fast starts

Rippled soles are good for indoor play.

and quick stops that volleyball demands.

There's a great deal of side-to-side movement, too. So be sure the toe area of the sneaker boasts extra reinforcing at the sides.

If you're going to be playing volleyball outdoors on an asphalt or cement court, buy sneakers with polyurethane soles. They last longer.

You don't need shoes for beach play, of course. You go barefooted.

The clothing you wear should not restrict your ability to move easily and comfortably. Shorts are worn in competitive play. Now that the forearm pass is an established feature of the game, more and more players are wearing long-sleeved shirts for the protection they offer.

Some players still prefer short-sleeved shirts, however. They like to be able to feel the ball strike their forearms when they bump it.

Uniforms often feature long-sleeved shirts; kneepads are a must.

There's no dispute about kneepads. Everyone wears them. They prevent painful scrapes and bruises.

Newer leather balls are softer and lighter than the older rubber ones. The panel seams are vulcanized instead of being sewn, which enables the ball to hold its shape longer.

The ball is usually white, although USVBA rules permit any light color for indoor play. The ball must be $25\frac{5}{8}$ to $26\frac{3}{8}$ inches (65 to 67 centimeters) in circumference, and weigh from 9 to 10 ounces (260 to 280 grams).

It should be inflated so as to rebound vertically from 60 to 65 inches when dropped from a height of 100 inches to a cement floor. Manufacturers' specifications, frequently stamped on the ball surface, usually provide for this.

The ball is soft and light, weighs less than a loaf of bread.

HOW THE GAME IS PLAYED

To volley, says the dictionary, is to return a ball before it hits the floor or ground.

And that's the whole idea of volleyball. Opposing teams hit the inflated ball back and forth across a high net until it bounces on the floor or ground, is hit out of bounds, or some other foul occurs.

A point is scored when the team receiving the serve fails to return the ball in the manner outlined by the rules. The first team to score 15 points wins the game.

The rectangular volleyball court is 59 feet (18 meters) long and 29½ feet (9 meters) wide.

A net, 3 feet, 3 inches (1 meter) wide, stretches across the center of the court, dividing it in half.

The top of the net is 7 feet, 4⅛ inches (2.2 meters) high for women and girls. (It's 7 feet 11⅝ inches or 2.4 meters high for men's games.)

There is a spiking line across each court 9 feet, 10 inches (3 meters) from the center line. Back-court players are not permitted to spike from within the area between the spiking line and the net.

There are six players on a team, three in the back half of the court (the right back, center back, and left back), and three in the front half (the right front, center front, and left front). The player in the right back position serves the ball.

If you play baseball or softball and you hold down the left field position, you're the left fielder

18

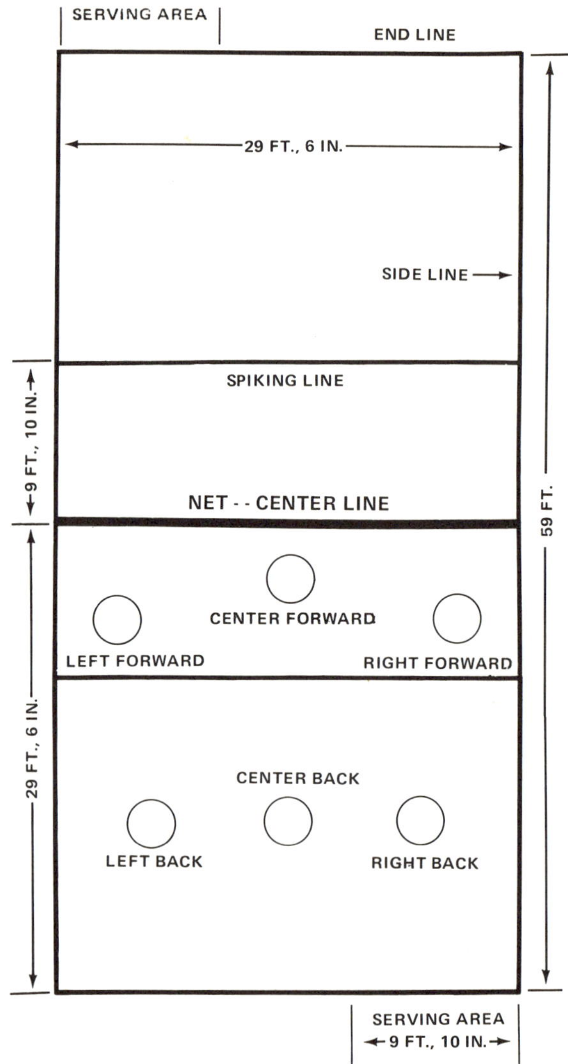

for the entire game. But in volleyball it's different. You play each position in turn. Whenever your team wins the right to serve, the players rotate one position in a clockwise direction. The "new" right back then serves.

There's a coin toss before the game begins. The team winning the toss can either serve or choose a particular side of the court on which to play. Usually the team that wins the toss decides to serve, because serving gives the team an opportunity to score.

The server, standing in the serving area behind the court's end line (see diagram), must hit the ball with her hand, fist, or arms over the net and into the receiving team's court. The serve cannot touch the net or a player on the serving team, and it must pass over the net between the two net antennas. The antennas are 2½ - to 3½-foot vertical rods that extend above the net at each end to indicate its outside boundaries. (They also assist the referee in determining whether the net has been touched during play.)

If the serve is not good, the referee calls for the opposition team to serve. This is called a "side out."

A player on the receiving team can hit the ball with her hands, fist, or arms; in fact, with any part of the body above and including the waist. No one is permitted to catch, scoop, lift, or throw the ball.

A team can hit the ball three times before sending it back over the net, but no more than three times.

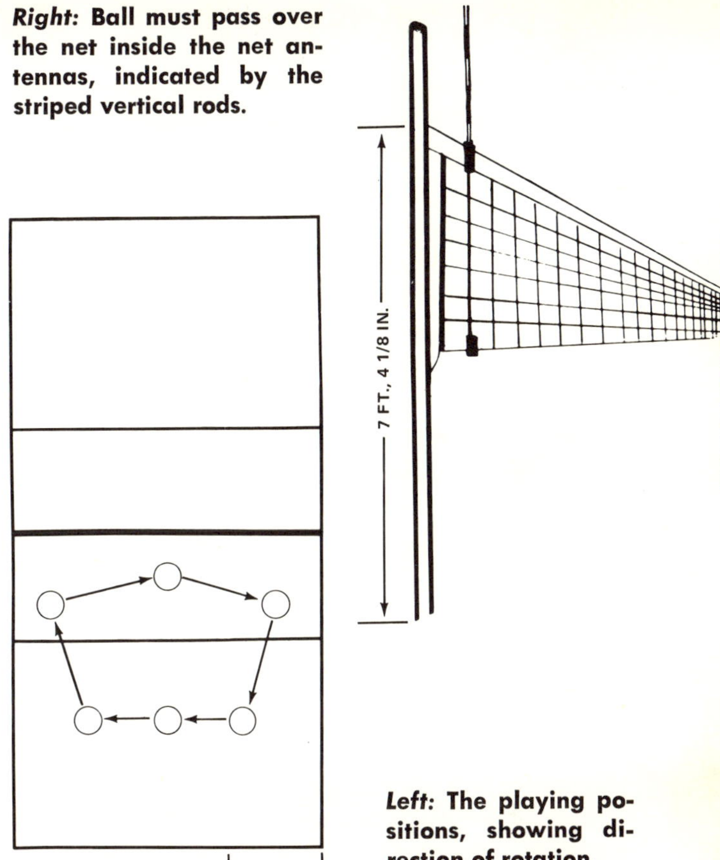

Right: Ball must pass over the net inside the net antennas, indicated by the striped vertical rods.

Left: The playing positions, showing direction of rotation.

If the ball touches a player accidentally, it counts as one of three hits. A player cannot make two successive hits. (An exception occurs when the ball comes over the net and you block it; then you are permitted to hit the ball a second time.)

Only the serving team can score. It earns one point each time the ball touches the floor in the receiving team's court. The serving team can also earn one point if a member of the receiving team hits the ball out of bounds or commits a foul.

The same person continues to serve after each point until her team makes an error or commits a foul, either of which results in a side out.

Any foul—that is, any violation of the rules—is penalized by a loss of a point if committed by the receiving team, or by a side out if committed by the serving team. These infractions are fouls:

• A player is out of position when the ball is served.

• A player contacts the net when the ball is in play.

• A player reaches over the net to play the ball (except when following through on a block or spike).

• A player crosses the center line while the ball is in play.

• A player positioned in the back court spikes in front of the spiking line.

• A team takes more than two time-outs during a game. (A time-out lasts a maximum of 30 seconds.)

Play is supervised by a referee who is stationed on a platform at one end of the net. The referee decides when a ball is in play, when it is dead, when a side is out, when a foul has been committed, and when a point has been scored.

Play is supervised by the referee.

The referee may be assisted by an umpire, stationed on the side of the court opposite the referee, and two or four linesmen. Stationed in the corners of the court, the linesmen indicate to the referee when a ball is "in" or "out."

The first team to score 15 points wins the game. But a team must win by at least 2 points. For example, if the score is 15 to 14, the game continues until one team gains a 2-point advantage over the other. The final score might be 17-15 or even 19-17.

In high school play, a match usually consists of a maximum of three 15-point games; that is, the first team to win two games wins the match.

There are many variations of volleyball's rules and regulations, and it would take a book at least the size of this one to explain them all.

JUNIOR PLAY—A version of volleyball for junior players (up to sixteen years of age) that calls for a net that is 7 feet high and a ball that weighs only 6 to 7 ounces. The server can stand in the center of the offensive court, instead of toward the corner. Two serves are permitted, not one.

There is no limit on the number of hits a team may use in playing the ball over the net, and any individual player is permitted to hit the ball twice in succession.

The size of the court used in junior play can vary with the number of players. It is 40 by 20 feet if there are six members on each team; 50 by 25 feet if there are nine players on a team; or 60 by 30 feet for teams of twelve players.

DOUBLES—This is a form of play between two pairs of players, that is, there are two players on each side. One position is designated as the left area; the other, the right area. The court is 30 feet wide and 50 feet long.

The first team to score 11 points, or whichever team is leading after five minutes of play, is the winner.

Doubles is the version of volleyball that is very popular on California beaches. The difficulty of defending a court that is almost full size with only two players is the chief reason why beach players look upon standard six-player basketball as a child's game.

There are women's, men's, and co-ed teams. The

Only the serving team can score.

last named are often called mixed teams.

One member of a team will seek to find a partner whose skills are complementary. A player who excels on the right side will look for a player who is best on the left side. A powerful spiker wants to be teamed with a good setter.

There are also special rules for co-ed competition, in which teams are made up of girls and boys. They are to be found in the section of this book titled "Co-ed Volleyball." The rules for beach volleyball can also be found in that section.

The official rules of volleyball are available in booklet form from the U.S. Volleyball Association (P.O. Box 77065, San Francisco, CA 94107). The rule book costs $2.50.

In Canada, competitive volleyball is supervised by the Canadian Volleyball Association (333 River Road, Vanier, Ontario K1L 8B9). A Canadian rule book costs $1.50.

For additional instructional information, and news and feature articles about volleyball and its leading teams and players, there are two publications you can read. One is *Volleyball Review*, published six times a year by the U.S. Volleyball Association (address above). A one-year subscription costs $3.

The other is *Volleyball Magazine* (Presidio Plaza, Santa Barbara, CA 93101). It is also published six times a year. A one-year subscription costs $9.

To stretch the muscles of the upper body, push with your hands while you keep your pelvis on the floor.

WARMING UP

Whether you play volleyball with a team in organized competition or play just for the fun of it at a beach or in the park, you should do some light exercises before the game begins. In recent years, trainers and coaches have come to realize the value of stretching exercises, such as those explained in this section, in preventing strains and sprains.

Begin by jogging. Three or four minutes of light running will help to get your heart and lungs going.

The first stretching exercise to try involves the muscles of your upper body. Stretch out on the floor, supporting your upper body with your hands. Straighten your arms but keep your pelvis on the floor.

Above and below: This exercise stretches the muscles of the lower back. Grasp the outer edges of your feet and bend your head to your legs.

Repeat the exercise, and the others described in this section, several times. If any exercise causes pain, don't do it.

Next, work on the muscles of the lower back. Sit on the floor with your legs extended. Raise your hands over your head and sweep them toward your feet. Grip the outer edges of your sneakers and bend your head downward.

For the upper back muscles, lie down on your back, your legs extended. Raise your legs up and over your head, keeping your hands and arms on the floor. Try touching your toes to the floor and resting them there.

To unlimber the muscles of the upper back, lie down, then raise your feet up and over your head.

This popular exercise stretches the big muscles in the backs of the legs. Keep your body straight and your heels to the floor as you lean.

24

To stretch the big muscles in the backs of your legs, stand about three or four feet from a wall and face it squarely. Keeping your body straight and your heels on the floor, put your hands on the wall and lean.

An exercise to stretch the muscles of the shoulders begins from a kneeling position. Tilt your upper body back so that you're sitting on your feet, placing your hands on the floor behind you. Then raise your knees and hold that position, balancing your weight on your hands.

These are just a few of the many stretching exercises you can do. Your coach probably has several others. They don't take long to do, but they're well worth the effort, for they make it much less likely that you'll suffer bothersome aches and pains.

By kneeling and balancing your weight on both hands, then raising your knees, you stretch your shoulder muscles.

HOW TO JUMP

If there is one "secret" toward achieving success in volleyball, it is the ability to jump. Being able to leap high into the air is important both offensively and defensively, that is, in spiking the ball and attempting to block when the opposition spikes.

There are many exercises and drills that you can perform to strengthen your leg muscles and thereby increase the height of your jumps. If you play for a school team, your coach will undoubtedly establish an exercise program for you and your teammates meant to increase your jumping ability. It's possible to boost the height of your jumps by three or four inches in just one season, if you work at it.

Remember, in volleyball, it's not how far you can jump that's important. You want to be able to jump vertically—straight up.

Running up flights of stairs is one good exercise. Even walking up stairs is helpful. Squatting, then standing, and doing it repeatedly, is another exercise that builds leg muscles.

Simple squat jumps are very good. Squat and jump. Do it again. Do it a third time, but on the third jump, try to leap as high as you can.

Another drill involves stringing a rope between two chairs so that it is about one foot above the floor. Jump over the rope from one side to the other and then jump back, and keep repeating the exercise for a period of two minutes.

Whether you're playing on offense or defense, you have to be ready to jump high.

Rest for two minutes, and then start jumping again for two minutes.

The drill consists of three two-minute periods of jumping, the periods interrupted by a rest period of two minutes.

Try to do the drill on a regular basis. Always be sure to warm up before you start jumping.

As you become proficient in going back and forth over the rope, reduce the rest period between the second and third periods of jumping. Instead of resting two minutes, reduce the period of rest to 1 minute, 30 seconds; then to 1 minute, 15 seconds; etc. You'll be building your stamina as well as increasing your jumping skill.

Another good exercise involves jumping against a wall and then noting the height of your jump each time. Stand several feet from the wall, facing it. Take two steps, plant both feet, and jump. Leap as high as you can, reaching with your fingertips.

Jump several times. Have a friend on a ladder mark the highest point you touch with a piece of adhesive tape. Or you can mark the wall yourself with a piece of chalk.

Then take ten jumps and try to touch the tape or chalk mark each time. Rest for 30 seconds and try ten more.

You can also jump up and try to touch the lower edge of a basketball backboard, which is 9 feet from the floor. Do it over and over. If the backboard is too high for you, try to leap up and touch the bottom edge of the net.

One drill involves jumping up against a wall, and checking the height of your jump with each try.

Your high school may have a weight-training device called a "Leaper." It can be used to increase your jumping skill by means of various toe raises, knee bends, leg presses, and other exercises. But never use the device unless you're being supervised by a coach or gym teacher.

Last, watch your weight. Nothing will hinder you more as a jumper than being overweight. Check your weight frequently during the season to be sure you haven't added any extra pounds.

HOW TO SERVE

When Japan's National Women's Team won the Olympic championship in 1976, some players were able to execute a steaming serve that jumped, swerved, and dropped as it came over the net. "The first time I saw it in use," recalls one American player, "I wasn't even able to touch it, let alone return it."

As this suggests, the serve is not merely a means of putting the ball in play. By hitting the ball hard, causing it to spin or drift to the right or left, or artfully placing it, you can make returning it difficult, maybe even impossible. In such a case, your team gets a point (called an ace).

If you're a beginner, however, don't worry about scoring points with your serves. Simply concentrate on getting the ball into the opposition court. Fail to do that and your team loses the ball; the opposition is awarded the serve.

Work on your accuracy before you try to get tricky. In one recent season, Lisa Fell, a seventeen-year-old senior at Hastings High School (Hastings-on-Hudson, New York), served 105 consecutive times without the ball once going out of bounds.

No one expects you to perform in that manner, of course. But if you don't get at least seven out of every ten of your serves within the boundaries of the opposition court, your value to your team is sure to be questioned.

The best way to practice serving is with a partner.

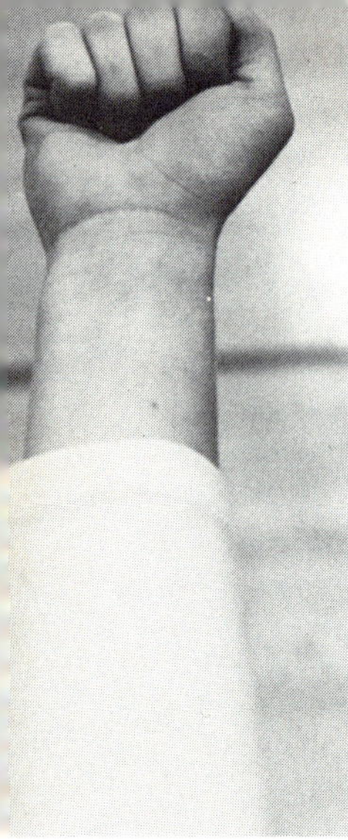 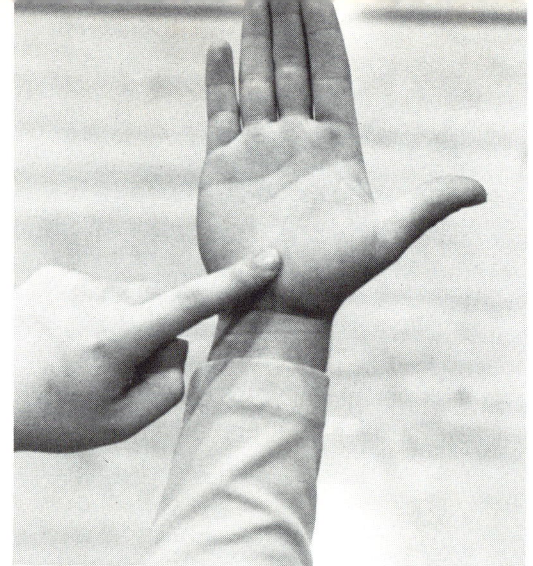

You stand on one side of the net; she stands on the other. You serve; she receives. Then reverse roles.

To help improve your accuracy, put a target in the opposition court—a towel, say—and try to hit it. Or try to place the ball precisely on the back-court line. Or a side line.

When you're receiving, always tell your partner when the ball is out of bounds. Indicate with your hands how far it was out. The next time she serves, she should adjust the power or direction of her serve.

The rules say that you, as a server, must stand within the 9-foot, 10-inch serving area and behind the end line or back-court line. How far behind is

Above: **For the underhand serve, you can use either your fist (keeping the thumb to the outside of the fingers) or your open hand, hitting with the heel.**

Below: **The underhand serve is easy. Simply swing your hand into the ball, keeping the arm and wrist straight. Be sure to follow through.**

up to you. If you feel your serve will be more effective by standing several feet in back of the line, do so.

You can't touch any of the lines that make up the serving area until you've made contact with the ball. Do so and it's a foot fault, and possession of the ball goes over to the opposition.

THE UNDERHAND SERVE—This is the easiest serve to learn. All you have to do is flip the ball from your left hand and hit it with your right fist or the heel of the right hand. If you're going to use your fist, keep the thumb to the outside of your index finger when you close your hand.

Stand facing the net, your right foot slightly ahead of your left. Bend both knees slightly.

Holding the ball in your left hand, take a long backswing with your right arm. It's like bowling, except there's no ball in your hand.

As you swing your hand into the ball, take a short step with your left foot (the rear foot). This step helps you to get power into the serve.

If you're using your fist, strike the ball with the knuckles and the heel of the hand at the same time. If you are going to keep your hand open, strike with the heel of your hand. In either case, what you must do is present a perfectly flat surface to the ball as you hit it.

Be sure to follow through. This means to continue the upward swing of your hand after you've made contact. Don't let the hand veer off to the right or left. If you do so, the ball is likely to go out of bounds.

It's also important to keep your eyes on the ball. If you look up before the hand makes contact, you're very likely to see a bad serve.

No matter how you serve—underhand or overhand— keep your eyes on the ball until you've made contact.

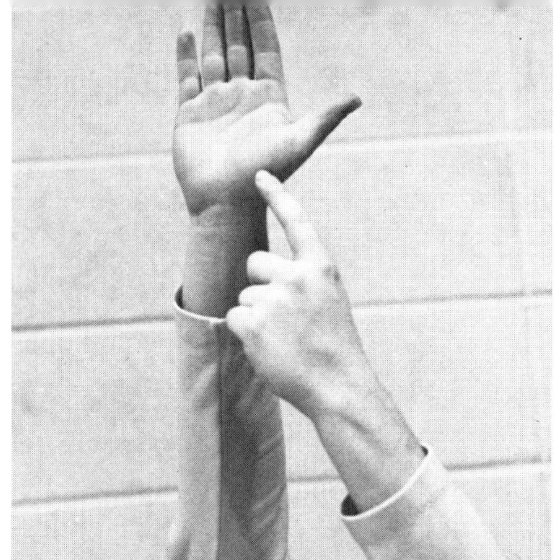

For the overhand serve, it's best to use an open hand, hitting with the heel.

THE OVERHAND FLOATER—The underhand serve usually travels lazily and in a high arc, which makes it easy to return. The overhand floater is a more effective weapon.

When you use the overhand floater and you hit the ball right, it soars through the air without any spin. This causes it to act unpredictably. It may drop, rise, or whip from side to side with a fishtail effect.

You can use your fist, hitting the ball with the heel of the hand and the knuckles simultaneously. But it's better to use your open hand and make contact with the heel. The open hand method gives you greater accuracy.

The overhand floater. First, get set, then toss the ball straight up.

Face the net. Hold the ball in your left hand. Put your left foot ahead of your right. Get comfortably balanced.

Toss the ball about two or three feet straight up

30

into the air, keeping it just in front of your left shoulder.

Cock your right arm behind your body. Bring it forward as the ball starts to fall. Keep your wrist firm.

Make contact with the heel of your hand at a point just below the center of the ball. You have to hit below the center in order to send the ball up and over the net.

There's little follow-through. It's almost as if you simply jabbed the ball.

One other piece of advice: How you position the

Cock the right arm, then drive the right hand into the ball. There's little follow-through.

Make contact just below the ball's center.

spot on the ball that encloses the valve stem has an effect on how the ball travels. For example, if you point the valve stem down, the ball will break with a downward curve. Point the valve stem directly toward your target, and the ball will veer from side to side. Always check how the valve stem is positioned before you make your toss.

ADVANCED SERVES—Almost all high school players use either the underhand serve or the overhand floater. Two other serves you may hear about are the overhand spin serve and the roundhouse serve. But these are for experienced players.

In the overhand spin serve, the hand (never the fist) rolls over the top of the ball as contact is made. This gives topspin to the ball, causing it to drop abruptly as it goes over the net. As you can imagine, it can be an effective piece of strategy.

The roundhouse serve gets its name from the windmill pattern the arm traces as the serve is executed. You can really club the ball when you use a roundhouse serve. There's both a roundhouse floater and a roundhouse spin serve. When beginners try such serves, they usually have much difficulty controlling them.

A roundhouse serve by Kimie Morita of the Japanese National Women's Team.

PLACING THE SERVE

Once you've developed skill as a server and are able to keep the ball within the court boundaries consistently, you can think about placing the ball, sending your serves to the area where the opposition is the most vulnerable.

It's usually best to place the ball as deep in the opposition court as you can. A deep serve forces the player receiving the ball to back up, and her pass isn't likely to be a very good one as a result.

Also, when the ball goes deep, the receiver may decide that it's going out of bounds and make no effort to return the ball. If the ball should remain in bounds, you've then scored a point.

The best placement of all is usually deep along the side line to your right (to the opposition left back, that is). The receiver then has to decide whether the ball is in bounds in terms of both the side line and the back line.

If she decides the ball is in bounds, she then must play it toward the center net area. This means, in turn, that the setter will probably have to set up the left forward spiker. Your teammates, anticipating this sequence of play, will be ready to block.

A serve can also be effective when sent diagonally across the court, toward the right back. Again, the receiver will have to return the ball toward the center net area.

If you're playing a team that is well known to

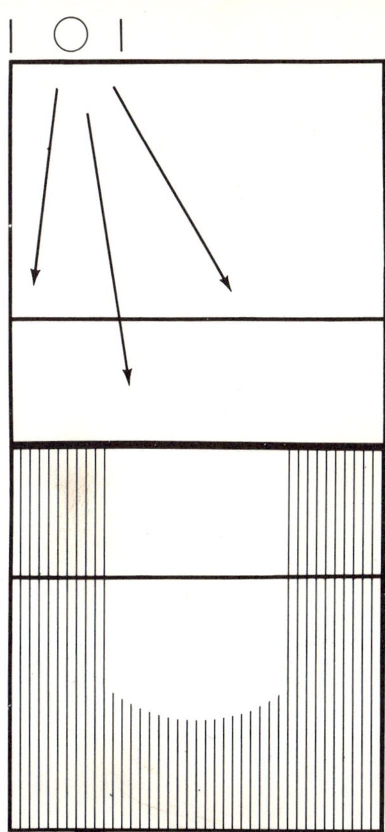

Shaded area indicates where you can try to place the ball.

you, consider how the opposition players are positioned before your serve. Try to send the ball to any player you know to be a weak returner.

HOW TO PASS

In modern volleyball, with its fast pass-set-spike sequence of play, the pass is the method used to get the ball to the setter.

The standard pass used today is called the bump pass, or, simply, the bump. You "bump" the ball off your forearms.

The bump became popular during the 1960s. Before it was introduced, players used a two-hand chest pass, letting the ball rest momentarily on their fingertips, then snapping it away. The bump is an improvement because you never get called for illegally catching the ball when you use it. That sometimes happened in the case of the two-hand pass.

When putting your forearms together for a bump pass, first join your hands. There are at least three different ways to do this, and they are described in the paragraphs below. Try each method and then use the one that is the easiest and most comfortable.

One method calls for you to first make a fist with each hand and place your thumbs side by side. Then wrap the fingers of one hand around the fingers of the other.

Or try this: Place your palms and thumbs together and lightly interlock your fingers. Then bend

The bump pass; create a flat rebounding surface with your forearms.

your wrists so your fingers point to the floor.

A variation is to place the palms, thumbs, and index fingers together, and then lightly interlock the remaining fingers. Bend your wrists so the index fingers point to the floor.

As stated above, it doesn't make much difference which method you use. The important thing to do is create a perfectly flat surface out of your forearms.

When the ball comes to you, make contact with your wrists or lower forearms. All you want to do is "bump" the ball gently. There's seldom any need to whack it hard.

It's important to get to the spot where the ball

Three methods of joining your hands when bumping: Wrap the fingers of one hand around the other fist (left); place the palms and thumbs together and lightly interlock the fingers (center); place the palms, thumbs, and index fingers together, and interlock the remaining fingers.

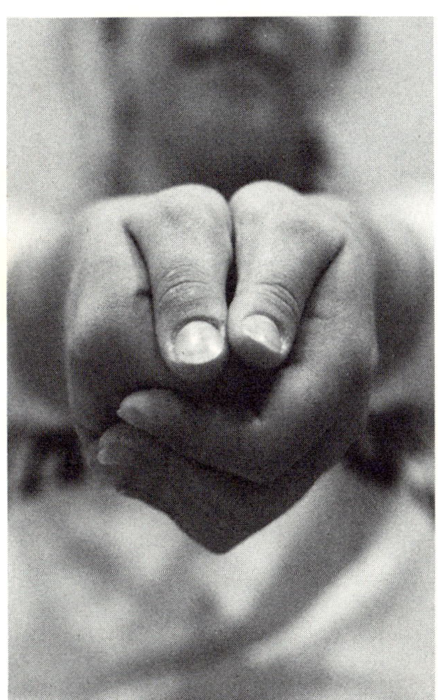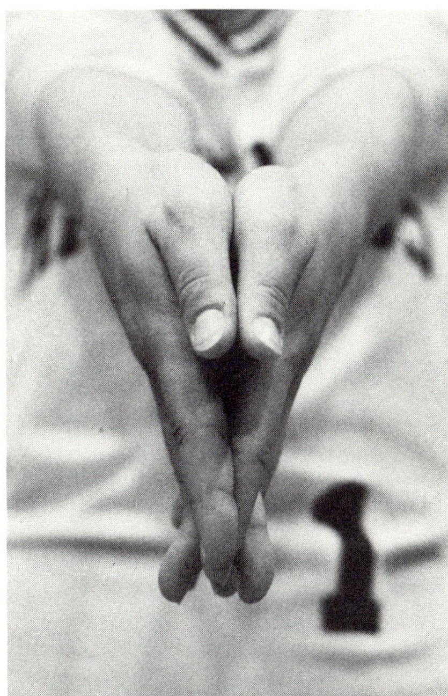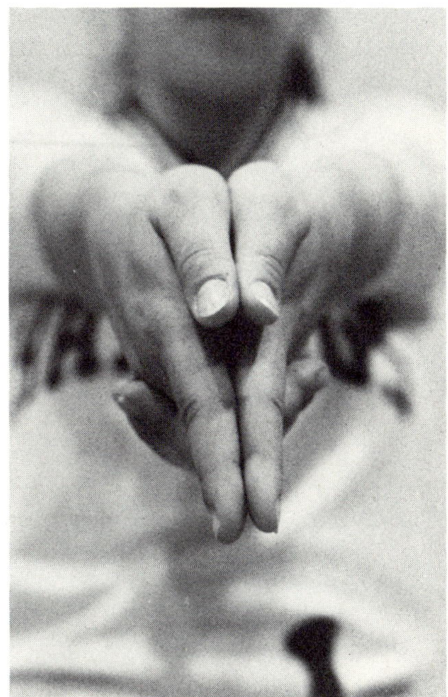

is coming down. Bend in the knees; get down low. Let the ball come to you. As it makes contact, straighten your legs.

How much you follow through with your forearms depends on how fast the ball is traveling and how far you intend to pass it. If it's a slow-moving ball and you want to pass it a good distance, you'll have to swing your forearms high to get power and direction into the pass. But if the ball comes ripping toward you, you may not use any follow-through at all, but simply allow the ball to carom off your forearms.

Get down low to receive the ball; rise up when you bump it away.

Practice the bump every day. Bump the ball against a wall. When it rebounds, bump it back. Or bump the ball straight up in the air, and bump it again when it comes down. When you have a partner to work with, bump the ball back and forth across the net.

PASSING TO THE SIDE—You should not only learn how to pass the ball forward, but also to your right and left. Suppose you're passing to the left. Dip your left shoulder and tilt your forearms to the left, so they'll send the ball in that direction.

BACKWARD PASS—Sometimes you'll be called

In executing a backward pass, lunge forward and get under the ball, and send it back over your head.

Here the pass goes to the setter (right), breaking toward the center net area.

upon to make a backward pass. You'll be facing away from the net and have to send the ball back over your head, and perhaps over the net, too. This situation occurs when the ball glances off a blocker's fingertips and goes whizzing into the back-court area.

Line up your shoulders so they're parallel with the gym's back wall. Throw your hips forward as the ball passes over your head and you move to make contact. This will enable you to send the ball high. You have to get it up into the air or it won't clear the net.

Whether you're passing back, forward, or to one side, it's vital that you keep your eyes on the ball. Don't let yourself be distracted by the teammate who is to receive the ball. You must watch the ball right up until the time it contacts your forearms.

ONE-HAND PASSING—Since volleyball is such a

fast-moving, even frantic game, you're not always going to be able to get into position to execute a pass with both forearms. There's only time to lash out and hit the ball with one arm.

Keep the arm straight. You can either make a fist or use your open hand.

Get down low. Watch the ball carefully.

Play the ball off your wrist or at a point just above it. Simply try to poke the ball up into the air so a teammate can make a follow-up play.

Communicating is essential to success in passing; in fact, you should never move to hit the ball, whether you're passing or setting, without first letting your teammates know your intentions.

When you're getting ready to bump, shout out, "My ball!" or "Mine!" or, simply, "Me!" Really blast it out. Keep repeating it until you're sure everyone has gotten the message.

If a teammate is closer to the ball than you are and in a better position to execute the pass, then shout out, "Yours!"

If a teammate goes outside the court boundaries to retrieve a ball (which is perfectly legal), and you go with her, shout, "I'm here!" or "With you!" In this way, you're letting her know that you're there to receive the pass.

Suppose you're playing the center back position. A ball is driven right in between you and the right back (the player on your right as you face the net).

Who should take the ball?

Such situations should be discussed before the game begins. In the case above, the ball in question would probably be your responsibility, since it is likely to be easier for you to move to your right and get the ball than it is for your teammate to move to her left. But it's something the two of you should work out together.

If you're the center back, it also might be easier for you to recover balls that are sent deep behind the right back. But in order to be able to do so, you'll have to have an arrangement with your teammate that she doesn't go back for them.

Even though you do such strategic planning, you should still call for the ball every time. Without communication, there's chaos.

HOW TO SET

The spiker with her searing drives never fails to draw oohs and aahs from the spectators. But setting is just as important as spiking. Even more so. Indeed, were it not for the setter's high and gentle tosses, the spiker would never be able to slam the ball effectively.

Setting is not easy. It requires skills unlike those encountered in any other sport.

It's illegal to catch the ball, of course. But when you set up a spiker, you first have to position your hands almost as if you *were* going to catch it. Then, just as the ball arrives, you flick it away.

Setting is also difficult because of the mental pressure involved. A good setter has the ability to see the approaching ball and the opposition players at the same time—and then set the ball accordingly. "The setter is like a quarterback," says one coach. "She decides who the spiker is going to be and where the spiked ball should go. In other words, she calls the play."

THE FRONT SET—Get in position first. For a front set, this means getting under and just behind the ball and waiting for it to come down.

Tilt your head back and hold your hands in front of your forehead. Spread the fingers. Your thumbs

Setter flips the ball high above the net for advancing spiker.

As you get ready to set, spot the ball through a "window" formed by your hands.

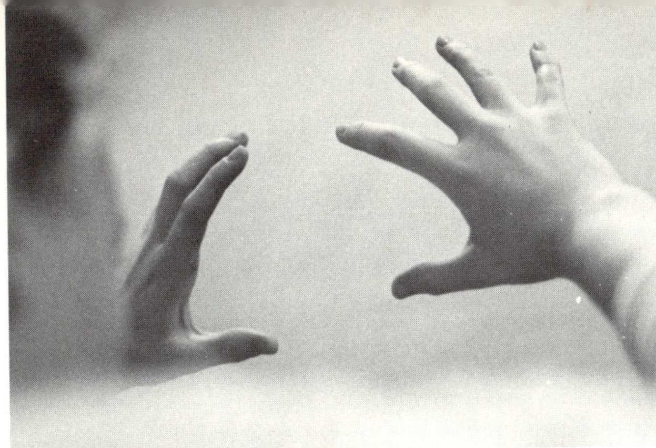

should be two or three inches apart. You should be looking at the ball as it drops toward you through the "window" formed by your thumbs and index fingers.

As the ball drops toward you, "give" a little with your hands, elbows, and knees. Receive the ball on your fingertips. (Imagine that you're going to leave your fingerprints on the ball's surface.) Don't let the ball touch your palms.

Thrust the ball up into the air, straightening your fingers, wrists, and arms. It's a very quick movement. Just snap the ball away.

How high you send the ball depends on the type

***Right:* The front set; as soon as the ball arrives, snap it away.**

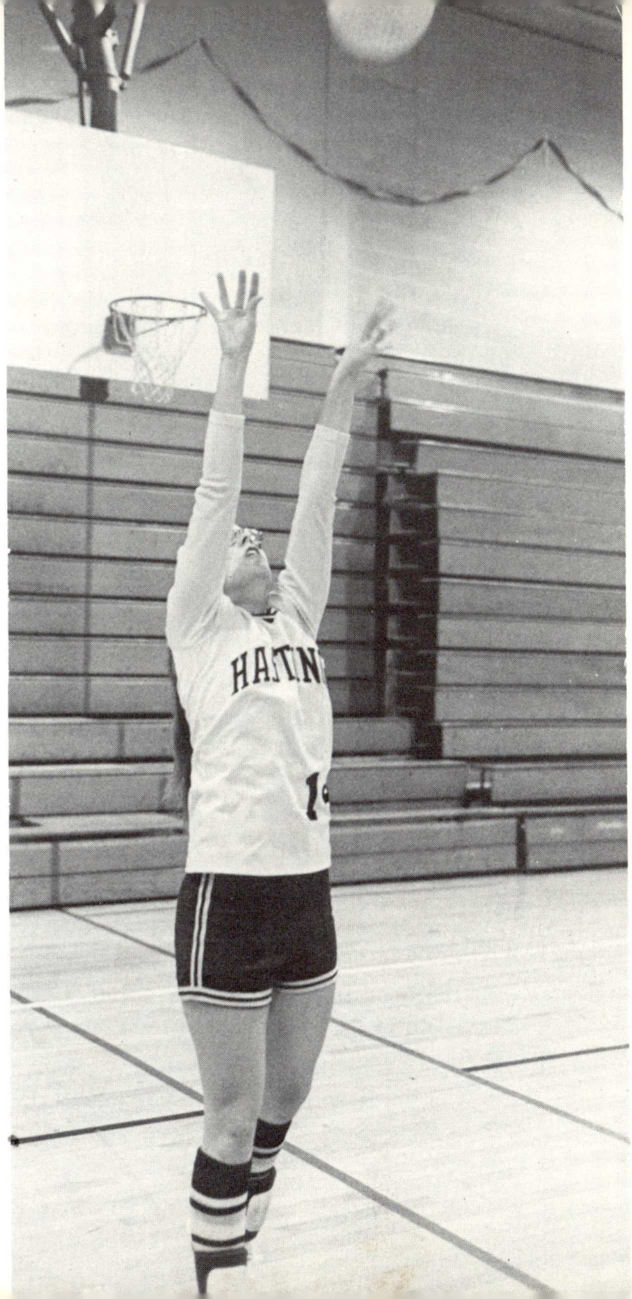

of play involved. Sometimes you'll want to send the ball straight up into the air so it goes several feet higher than the net. Other times you'll want to toss the ball up only to a point just above the top of the net.

The Japanese national men's and women's teams introduced this type of set in the mid-1960s. Japanese players are smaller in stature than those of many other nations. The low vertical set was developed to enable a shorter-than-average player to spike the ball hard.

You can practice setting with yourself or a partner. Set the ball straight up in the air, then "re-set" it when it comes down. You can set the ball against a wall and set it again when it rebounds. Practice setting from a kneeling position and while sitting. During a game, there may be times when you have to set the ball from these positions.

Another way to practice setting is by flicking the ball toward a basketball rim. Stand close to the backboard. Toss the ball toward the rim. When it comes back down, let it land on your fingertips and snap it back up, trying to hoop it.

If you have a partner to work with, set the ball back and forth. Put variety into your practice sessions. For instance, when the ball comes to you, self-set it; that is, set it straight up into the air. Drop to your knees. When the ball comes down, set it to your partner from a kneeling position.

THE SIDE SET—When you're facing the net (or your back is to it), and the spiker is positioned to your left or right, you'll have to use a side set to get the ball to her.

If you want to set the ball to your left, drop the

When setting to the left, dip the left shoulder.

left shoulder. When the ball arrives, flick it away in that direction.

The Back Set—Suppose your body is positioned so that the spiker is behind you. You'll have to send the ball back over your head to get the ball to her. This is called a back set.

As the ball drops toward you, use the same body position as for the front set. But arch your back more and contact the ball above your forehead. Flick it up and back over your head.

No matter what type of set you're using, always call out the name of the teammate you're setting for. If the set is going to Monica, then shout out, "Monica! Monica!" as you move into position under the ball.

For the back set, bend your head back; arch your back.

Flo Hyman (No. 7), at 6-foot-5, is famed spiker for U.S. Women's National Volleyball Team.

HOW TO SPIKE

The spike is volleyball's most spectacular play. The spiker leaps high and slams the ball with all her power down into the opposition court. When it's done right, the ball is unreturnable.

Spikers are usually the tallest players on the team. But height isn't as important as jumping ability. The young woman who posed for the pictures in this section stood 5-foot-2, yet because of her ability to leap high she was able to get her spiking hand well above the net and hit the ball down.

Timing is just as important as the ability to jump. Most beginners have a tendency to jump too soon. They're going up at the same time the ball is going up. And they're back down on the floor when they should be up there hitting.

Wait until the ball has started to fall back down before you go up. Only in that way will you be able to get a solid hit.

Often the spike begins with a two- or three-step takeoff. The last step should bring you close to the net. Plant your feet and leap up.

You must spring upward, not forward. It's like the approach you use when executing a dive from a springboard. You approach the end of the board, plant both feet, and spring straight up into the air (and land back down on the board).

Remember to keep slightly in back of the ball. If you're directly under it when you go up, you're almost certain to drive the ball out of bounds.

Arch your back as you go up. Draw your right arm back, cocking it behind your head.

Spiker watches as ball is set. (See next photos.)

Still watching the ball, she drives for the net, leaps high, and slams the ball home.

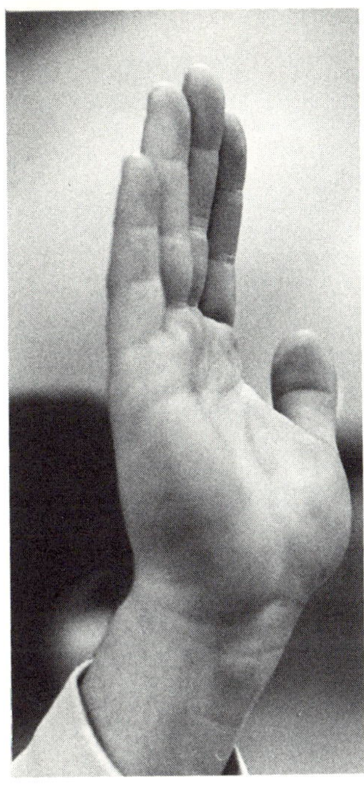
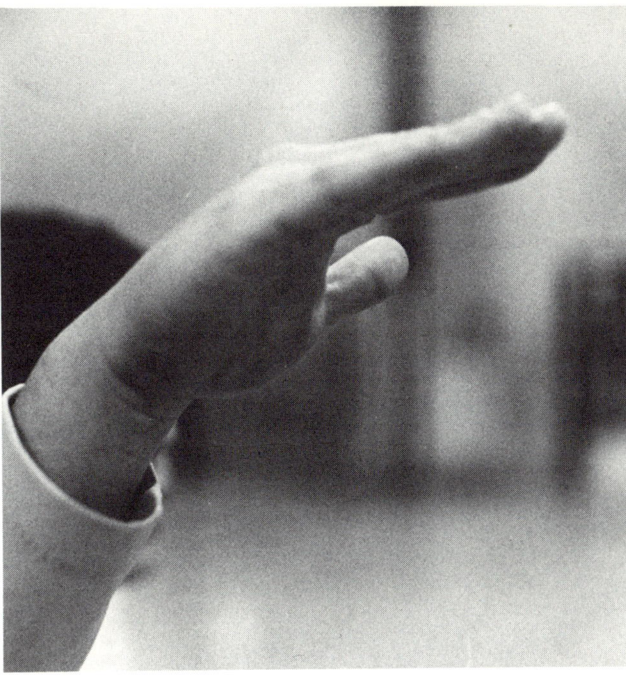

When you spike, it's important to try to hit the ball down. Your fingers flip forward to strike at or near the top of the ball.

When you sweep your arm forward and slam the ball, keep your hand open, the fingers together.

Hit the ball *down*. This means you have to hit the ball at or near the top, breaking your wrist so the fingers and palm come forward.

Once you begin to feel confident as a spiker, try placing your drives. Glance into the opposition court before beginning your approach to see how the players are positioned. Then determine where you're going to place the ball. But once you begin your approach, keep your eyes on the ball and don't take them off of it until you've made contact.

If you're on the right side of the court as you're getting set to spike, try targeting on or near the side line. That's more effective than sending the ball diagonally across the court. If you're on the left side of the court and get an opportunity to spike, keep the ball near the left side line.

Spiking drill: Bounce the ball in front of you so it rebounds about chest high; leap in the air and smash it down.

Anytime you spike and your hand crosses over the top of the net as you follow through, that's all right; it's not a foul. Of course, if your hand or any part of your body touches any part of the net, your team loses a point or the serve.

There are a couple of drills you can perform to improve your spiking skill. To sharpen your jumping ability—that is, to assure that you're learning to jump straight up and not forward—practice jumping in front of a wall. Take a two-step approach, plant both feet about 18 inches from the wall, and then leap. Thrust both arms over your head to add to your momentum. Perform the drill at a slow pace first, gradually increasing your speed.

To train yourself to hit the ball down, bounce the ball in front of you, then, on one of its rebounds from the floor, leap up and smash it down. Really slam it. Make the ball rebound so high that it touches the gym ceiling.

Or you can practice spiking with a tennis ball drill. Holding a tennis ball in your spiking hand, take a two-step running approach toward the net. Plant both feet and leap up. Reach over the net and fire the tennis ball straight down. Throw hard. Make it bounce straight up. This drill helps you to get the idea of the arm and wrist action you must use when spiking the volleyball.

One final piece of advice: If your spike wins a point or earns your team the serve, turn to your setter and say, "Nice going."

THE DINK

The dink is a soft shot that, at the beginning, looks like a spike. It's used to catch the defense off guard.

The attacking player leaps into the air behind a ball that's been set up for her, and cocks her arm as if she's planning to pound home a spike. But instead of belting the ball, she merely pushes it lightly with her fingertips. The dink is a gentle breeze compared to a thunderbolt.

The attacker usually tries to push the ball over the blockers. It's surprising how frequently the dink is successful.

As a beginner, your coach will probably have you use two hands when you execute a dink. This gives better control.

Keep your hands open and your fingers spread. Make contact with your fingertips, pushing the ball into an undefended area. If there happens to be two or three players in front of you at the net attempting to block, there will be plenty of open space.

The same advice applies if you use one hand instead of two. Keep your fingers widely spread. Gently push the ball toward the target you've picked out.

Deception is vital in order for the dink to be successful. Your opponents have to be expecting a devastating spike. This means that you have to disguise the fact that the dink is coming, approaching and leaping just as if you were going to spike.

The dink is a soft shot, the ball resting on the finger-tips for just a fraction of a second.

Here's a one-hand dink. Flick the ball over the blocker's head.

You're playing exactly the same role as a pitcher who is delivering a change of pace. He has to use a fast-ball motion; otherwise, the batter will never be fooled.

Also, you can't use the dink too often. The greater the element of surprise, the greater your chances of success.

ON THE ATTACK

This is volleyball's basic strategy: When the serve comes across the net, the ball is passed to a setter, who is usually close to the net, and the setter feeds the ball to a spiker, who slams it home.

The best teams are composed of specialists. Some players are hitters, others setters, and still others,

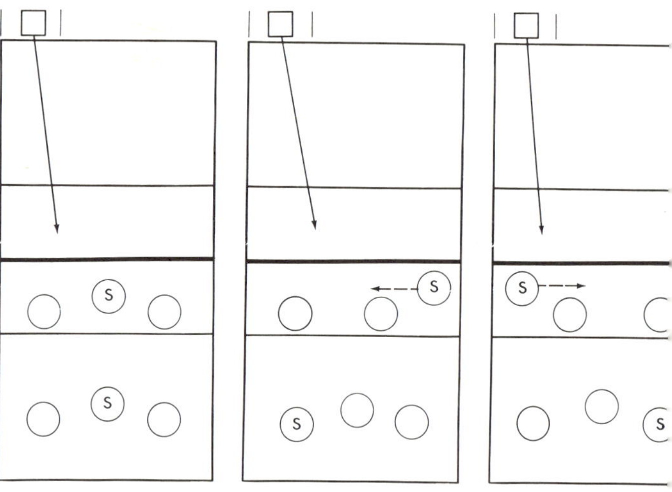

The 4-2 offense involves four spikers and two setters. When positioned in the front row at center net (diagram, left), setter (S) can feed either spiker. When positioned on either the right or left side, setter must dash to center net position as soon as server contacts ball.

spikers. Of course, a setter may spike the ball once in a while, and a spiker may set up a teammate, but usually players stick to the roles they've been assigned.

To further increase a team's efficiency, coaches align the players in a way that assures an effective attack. Many teams use a 4-2 alignment. In the 4-2, there are four players who can spike, and two players who are setters.

The 4-2 is also called the W formation because the alignment of the players, when viewed from the rear, resembles the letter W. And since it resembles an M when viewed from the front, some coaches refer to it as the M formation.

Whatever you call it, the two setters are always positioned opposite one another, one in the front row, one in the back row.

The setter in the front must be positioned in the center of the row so as to be able to feed the ball either backward or forward, giving variation to the team's attack.

It can happen, of course, that the setter will have to rotate to an outside position following the scoring of a point. In such cases, she must dart back to the center after the ball has been contacted on the serve. The rules permit her to remain there until the ball

Some coaches call the formation a W, others, an M. It depends on whether you're looking at it from the back or front.

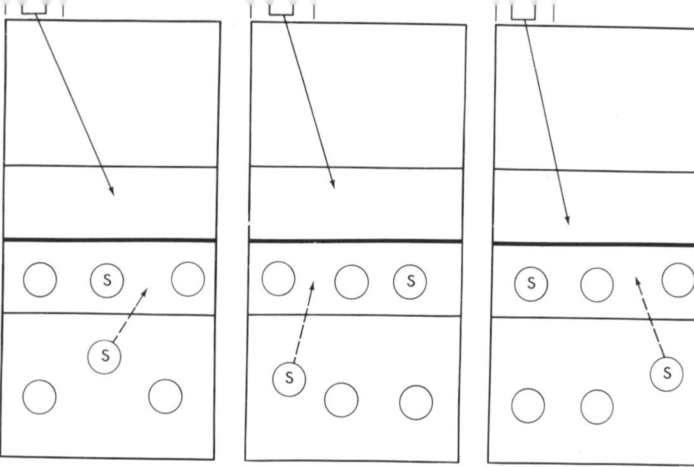

In what is called a 6-2 setup, setter (S) darts from back to front row as soon as ball is served.

is dead. Before the next serve, she must return to her regular position.

Other teams use what is called the 6-2 offensive system. In this, the setter always darts up to the net from the back court. Once there, she can feed any one of three spikers. A great variety of attacking variations are thus possible.

Awaiting the opponent's serve, players are coiled, ready to strike.

DEFENSIVE SKILLS

Anytime the opposition team is in possession of the ball, your team is the defensive team. Playing defense requires special skills.

When the ball is about to be served, get into a ready position. Face the server. Bend at the waist. Bend your knees. Your weight should be on the balls of your feet so you can move fast in any direction.

Don't let your hands hang down at your sides. You must be prepared to make contact with the ball, prepared to bump. This means your forearms should be in front of you and about parallel with the floor.

Defensive players are also often called diggers. Digging is hitting an opponent's serve or spike just

There's often only time to take a one-handed swipe at the ball.

Try to use your forearms when digging.

before the ball strikes the ground.

Whenever possible, use your forearms when digging. Sometimes, of course, you won't have any choice but to lash out with one hand or fist to make the save.

You'll also have to resort to a dig when one of your teammates drives the ball right into the net. The net "gives" and cushions the ball's impact, and it drops straight downward. Get down low and try to get your fists under the ball, popping it into the air so a teammate can spike.

HOW TO BLOCK

The block is volleyball's chief defensive play. One or more players leap into the air with upstretched arms in an effort to stop or deflect a spiked ball as it comes over the net. Any one or all of the players in the front line are permitted to block.

The job of blocking is not an easy one, chiefly because a spiked volleyball, according to recent tests, can be traveling at a speed of from 60 to 70 miles an hour.

But there are several things that you can do to swing the advantage to your favor. Skilled and aggressive blockers will sometimes score more than half of a team's points.

Good timing is vital. Most blockers jump too soon. They're going back down when the spiker is making contact. The ball sails over the tips of their fingers.

You should be moving into position when the spiker is getting ready to jump. Let her jump up first; then you jump.

Get right in front of the spiker. Keep your eyes on the ball. Raise your hands as high as you can as you go up.

Spread your fingers wide. The hands should be only a few inches apart. Keep your arms straight. You want them to act like fence posts.

If all goes well, the ball will smash into the heels of your hands and rebound to the floor on the

When you go up to block, spread your fingers; use both hands.

opposite side of the net. You'll also block balls with the fingers, palms, wrists, and forearms.

There's a rule that permits hands to go over the top of the net when blocking—and you should take advantage of it.

When you leap, reach over the net with your hands. This is sometimes called an attack block.

Be sure to reach over the net with your fingers—if you can.

You must get close to the net, but don't touch it.

Of course, you have to be careful and not touch the net. Should any part of your body contact the net, it's a foul. Your team loses a point or the serve as a result.

Usually a player touches the net because she has jumped forward, not straight up. Check the section in this book titled "How to Jump." It describes several drills you can do that will help you to become a straight-up jumper.

Another error that blockers make is permitting the ball to dribble down in front of their bodies on their side of the net. This is caused by being positioned too far from the net at the jump. If you concentrate on attack blocking, on getting your hands and wrists over the top of the net, this won't happen to you.

After the ball has been blocked, be alert for the next shot. If you were the one who blocked the

U.S. blockers leap high to stop a Japanese dink. No. 11 is Patty Dowdell, American defensive star.

ball, and it remains on your side of the net, the rules permit you to play it a second time.

Some experienced teams may use two or even three players against a block, with all the blockers leaping up at the same time. Their upstretched arms form a wall the spiked ball is almost sure to hit.

But in such cases, the other players must guard the areas of the court vacated by the blockers who have rushed to the net. Unless these "holes" are covered, the opposition is sure to exploit them.

How important is blocking? Consider this statistic: Patty Dowdell, star blocker for the U.S. Women's National Volleyball Team, scores as many as six or seven points a game with her blocking, according to her Coach, Arie Selinger.

DIVING AND ROLLING

Digging must often be combined with diving and rolling in order to be successful. In topflight high school competition, in fact, diving saves and rolling digs have become almost as much a part of the game as spikes and sets.

Don't attempt any diving unless you have strong forearms. Test your forearms with this exercise. Do a push-up, supporting your body with your toes and palms. Keep your forearms straight. Then have a teammate grasp your ankles and pick up your feet, raising them several inches. If your forearms cannot then support your body's weight, forget about diving. Push-ups are a good way to strengthen your forearms, incidentally.

Learn the correct diving technique on a mat and without any ball. Kneel on the mat and fall forward, landing on your hands, cushioning the impact by bending your elbows. Then squat and fall forward, again landing on your hands.

Now try diving forward from a squat. Leap forward, landing on your hands, not on your knees. Straighten the arms as soon as you've cushioned the impact of your landing.

Next, stand, bending deeply at the waist and knees, and try the exercise. Keep raising your upper

When you dive, you "save" yourself by landing on your hands. The elbows act like springs in cushioning the impact.

body until you're able to dive from an erect position. Always land on your hands; never let the knees touch first.

Now it's time to introduce the ball. As you take a two-step approach to the mat and dive, have a teammate toss you a soft lob. Hit the ball up into the air off of your forearms, then separate your hands and land on your palms. Repeat the drill over and over on the mat before you try digging and diving on a hardwood floor.

The dig-and-roll should also be first practiced on a mat before you attempt it on a gym floor. The "roll" in the dig-and-roll is a shoulder roll. You go from one shoulder over onto your back and then spring to your feet.

Try rolling over on a mat without the ball. From a squat, dip one shoulder, tuck your chin to your chest, and roll over on that shoulder, then onto your back, keeping your knees bent. Continue rolling until your feet contact the mat. Then push yourself to a standing position with your hands.

Of course, it has to be done smoothly and quickly. An accomplished player can roll over and come to her feet in about the time it takes you to snap your fingers.

When you're able to roll over smoothly and quickly, introduce the ball. Begin from a squat. Have a teammate toss you a soft lob. Leap forward, thrust your forearms out, and make contact with the ball. Then, tucking your hands to your chest, roll over and come to your feet.

In executing a dig-and-roll, you roll over on one shoulder.

End up on your feet.

CO-ED VOLLEYBALL

Volleyball is one of the small handful of sports in which teams are often composed of both girls *and* boys. If you've played volleyball on a beach or in a park, you already know this to be true. But many high schools are now providing programs for co-ed (short for coeducational) competition in volleyball.

The rules for co-ed volleyball are the same as those for regulation play, with these exceptions:

• Each team must consist of three boys and three girls.

• The sequence of serving must alternate—girl, boy, girl, boy, etc.

• Whenever the ball is hit by more than one player on a team, one of the players must be a girl. In other words, one boy cannot hit the ball before or after another boy.

• When a team's front line consists of two girls and a boy, a back-court player is permitted to block. (On an all-girl or all-boy team, only the three front-line players can block).

As mentioned earlier, professional volleyball teams representing the International Volleyball Association are co-ed, too. But pro teams have only two women players, not three. And they're usually setters and defensive specialists. Male players enjoy the glory of spiking.

There are also different rules for beach volley-

Many high schools now offer volleyball competition with teams made up of both girls and boys.

ball. The net is set at 7 feet, 9 inches when the sand is soft and loose. It's set at 7 feet, 10 inches on hard-packed sand. If girls play with a net at either one of these levels, it's not likely at all that they'll be able to spike. They'll be setting.

The ball used in beach play is heavier than the indoor ball, so it will be more likely to stay on course in the wind. The ball is made of rubber.

Because of the wind, serving is more difficult. You have to judge the direction of the wind before you hit the ball, and adjust accordingly. If the wind is blowing toward you, your serve has to be hit harder than normal, and you need a delicate touch if it is blowing away from you.

Since there's no ceiling overhead, some players like to rocket the ball high into the air when they serve. This is called a "sky ball." An indoor player may not know how to cope with a ball that comes plummeting straight down out of a sun-filled sky.

As multiples of five points are recorded, teams change courts. For example, teams would change at a score of 3-2, again at 7-3, and again at 11-4, etc. Switching courts is done to cancel the sun or wind advantage one team might have.

While six-player teams are often seen on beaches, teams of four and three players are also common. Doubles play (two players to a team) is also popular.

There's one other difference you may notice right away. It's harder to judge the ball's height and distance. This is because there are no objects to which

In New York's Central Park, volleyball teams are almost always co-ed.

Deep beach sand cushions rolls and dives.

the ball can be related, no walls or windows, no pillars or posts—just blue sky. It may take you a few games to get used to this lack of perspective.

This is not a big problem, however. If you're used to playing the game only indoors, you're sure to find beach volleyball a real treat. The deep beach sand serves as a soft cushion, and you'll find yourself diving for balls you'd never think of trying to retrieve in the gym. And, since there are no walls or ceilings for the ball to hit, it's much easier to keep it in play for long rallies.

GLOSSARY

ACE—A point scored as the direct result of a serve.

ANTENNA—Either of the two 2½- to 3½-foot vertical rods that extend above the net on each end to indicate its outside boundaries.

ATTACK BLOCK—A type of block in which the blocker reaches over the top of the net with her hands in an effort to deflect the ball downward.

BACK COURT—The area between the end line and the spiking line.

BLOCK—The effort by one or more players to reflect or stop an opponent's shot.

CANADIAN VOLLEYBALL ASSOCIATION—The governing body of amateur volleyball in Canada.

CENTER LINE—The line directly beneath the net that divides the court in half.

CO-ED—Competition in which teams are made up of both girls and boys; short for coeducational.

COURT—The area on which volleyball is played.

DEFENSIVE TEAM—The team that does not have possession of the ball.

DIG—To hit the ball just before it strikes the floor.

DINK—A softly placed shot, often used when the opposition is expecting a spike.

DOUBLES—A game played with only two players on each team.

END LINE—Either of the two boundary lines at either end of the court.

FLOATER—A type of serve in which the ball travels without any spin, dropping, rising, or whipping from side to side as it crosses the net.

FOOT FOUL—A violation of the rules that occurs when a player's foot touches a boundary line of the court as a serve is being made.

FOUL—A violation of the rules which results in the loss of the serve if committed by the serving team. If the foul is committed by the receiving team, it results in the scoring of a point by the serving team.

FRONT COURT—The area of the court from the spiking line to the net.

HELD BALL—A foul that occurs when the ball comes to rest in a player's hands or on the arms or other part of the body.

INTERNATIONAL VOLLEYBALL ASSOCIATION (IVA)—A league of professional volleyball teams, founded in 1975.

INTERNATIONAL VOLLEYBALL FEDERATION (IVBF)—An organization of volleyball associations in more than one hundred nations; drafts and publishes international rules and organizes and promotes world championship tournaments.

KILL—A spike.

LINE BALL—A ball that lands on one of the boundary lines.

LINESMAN—One of two or four officials who assists the referee in determining when a ball is in or out of bounds.

MATCH—Competition over a maximum of three games, which ends when one team wins two games.

OFFENSIVE TEAM—The team in possession of the ball; the attacking team.

PASS—A ball that is hit by one player to a teammate.

RALLY—A sequence of play in which the ball is repeatedly hit back and forth across the net until the serving team scores a point or loses the right to serve.

REFEREE—The chief official of a game who is stationed on a platform at one end of the net, and who is responsible for the conduct of the game, for enforcing the rules, for permitting time-outs, and penalizing rule infractions.

ROTATE, ROTATION—The clockwise movement of players when the team receives the ball for serving.

ROUNDHOUSE—A type of serve that is executed with a powerful overhand, straight-arm motion.

SAVE—To prevent the opposition from scoring a point or being awarded the serve by hitting the ball to a teammate just before it strikes the floor.

SERVE—To put the ball in play by hitting it over the net.

SERVING AREA—The area, 9 feet, 10 inches in width, just behind the end line at each end of the court, from which the ball is served.

SET, SETUP—To toss the ball into the air for a teammate so that it can be effectively spiked.

SETTER—The player who passes the ball up into the air, usually close to the net, so it can be spiked by a teammate.

SIDE OUT—The loss of service by a team.

SKY BALL—In beach volleyball, a type of serve hit very high into the air so it drops straight down into the opposition court.

SPIKE—To drive the ball downward into the opposition court, usually from the top of a jump.

SPIKING LINE—A line across each court 9 feet, 10 inches from the center line. Back-court players are not permitted to spike from within the area between the spiking line and the net.

UMPIRE—The official who assists the referee and is stationed on the side of the court opposite the referee.

UNITED STATES VOLLEYBALL ASSOCIATION (USVBA)—The chief governing body of volleyball; establishes volleyball rules, promotes tournaments, and certifies officials.

VOLLEY—To return a ball before it hits the floor or ground.

YOUNG MEN'S CHRISTIAN ASSOCIATION (YMCA)—A worldwide service organization, founded in 1844, providing programs to improve physical and mental health.